Frog

Written by Stephen Savage

Illustrated by Phil Weare

Thomson Learning
New York

OBSERVING NATURE

Ant   Duck

Butterfly   Frog

First published in the
United States in 1995 by
Thomson Learning
115 Fifth Avenue
New York, NY 10003

First published in
Great Britain in 1994 by
Wayland (Publishers) Ltd.

Library of Congress Cataloging-in-
  Publication Data
Savage, Stephen.
  Frog / written by Stephen Savage;
illustrated by Phil Weare.
      p.   cm.—(Observing nature)
  Includes index.
  ISBN 1-56847-326-5
  1. Frogs—Juvenile literature.
2. Frogs—Life cycles—Juvenile
literature. [1. Frogs.] I. Weare, Phil, Ill.
II. Title. III. Series: Savage, Stephen,
1965- Observing nature.
QL668.E2S26   1995
597.8'9—dc20   94-31200

Printed in Italy

Contents

What Is a Frog?

Frogs are amphibians, which means they can live on land and in water. Their long back legs are good for hopping, and their webbed feet are good for swimming.

If you see a frog or toad, this is how you can tell them apart. Most frogs have shiny skin that is smooth and slimy. Most toads have dry lumpy skin, shorter back legs, and usually walk instead of hop.

common frog

common
toad

5

Hibernation

Frogs are cold-blooded. This means that their bodies are the same temperature as the air. In the winter when the weather is very cold, most frogs hide away and go to sleep. This sleep is called hibernation.

The frogs will not wake up to eat until the warmer
weather in the spring. Even if you do not have a pond,
you may have a frog hibernating in your backyard.

What Do Frogs Eat?

Frogs have good eyesight for hunting the small animals that they eat. They can catch insects, spiders, slugs, and earthworms using their long sticky tongues.

8

A frog may use
its front feet to
clean dirt off an
earthworm before
swallowing it.

Frogs have very wide mouths,
but they have very small teeth, and
only in the upper jaw. When a frog swallows,
its large eyes press down into its head. This helps the frog
swallow a large meal. Frogs can catch food only on land.

Returning to the Pond

Not long after the frogs awaken from their sleep, they return to the pond where they grew up. This may be a pond in the country, a ditch, a village pond, or even a small backyard pond.

The male frogs reach the pond first, and their croaking sounds can be heard all around. This croaking sound warns other male frogs to stay away. It may also attract female frogs.

Frog Spawn

Although frogs can live on land, they have to lay their eggs in water. Mating takes place when the female frogs arrive at the pond. Many types of frogs lay their eggs in a large mass of jelly. Toads often lay their eggs in a string of jelly. Both kinds of eggs are called spawn.

toad spawn

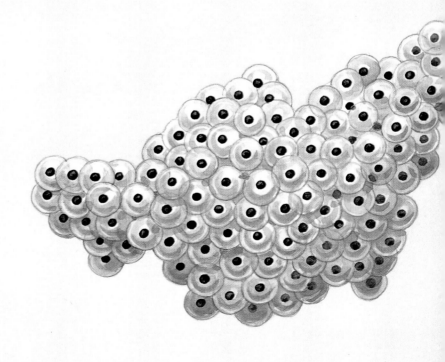

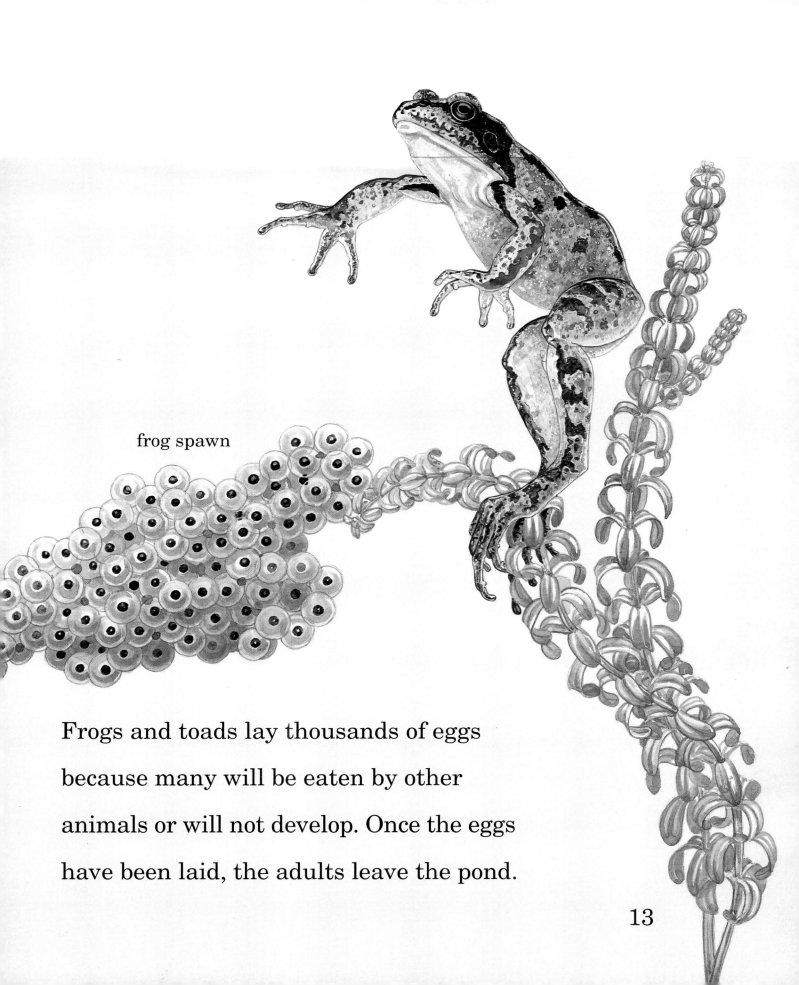

frog spawn

Frogs and toads lay thousands of eggs
because many will be eaten by other
animals or will not develop. Once the eggs
have been laid, the adults leave the pond.

13

The Eggs Hatch

The black dot in the center of each egg slowly develops and changes shape to become a tadpole. After two weeks the tadpoles are ready to hatch. At first, the tadpole cannot swim very well and uses its sucker mouth to hang on to pond plants.

After a few days, the tadpole grows feathery gills that allow it to breathe underwater like a fish. The tadpole's mouth changes shape so that it can eat algae and other pond plants.

Enemies in the Pond

diving beetle

sticklebacks

water-boatman

The pond is full of danger and many of the tadpoles will
be eaten by other pond animals. Dragonfly larvae lurk in
the pondweed and catch any tadpoles that come near.
Water boatmen, diving beetles, and sticklebacks will
often chase and catch tadpoles.

16

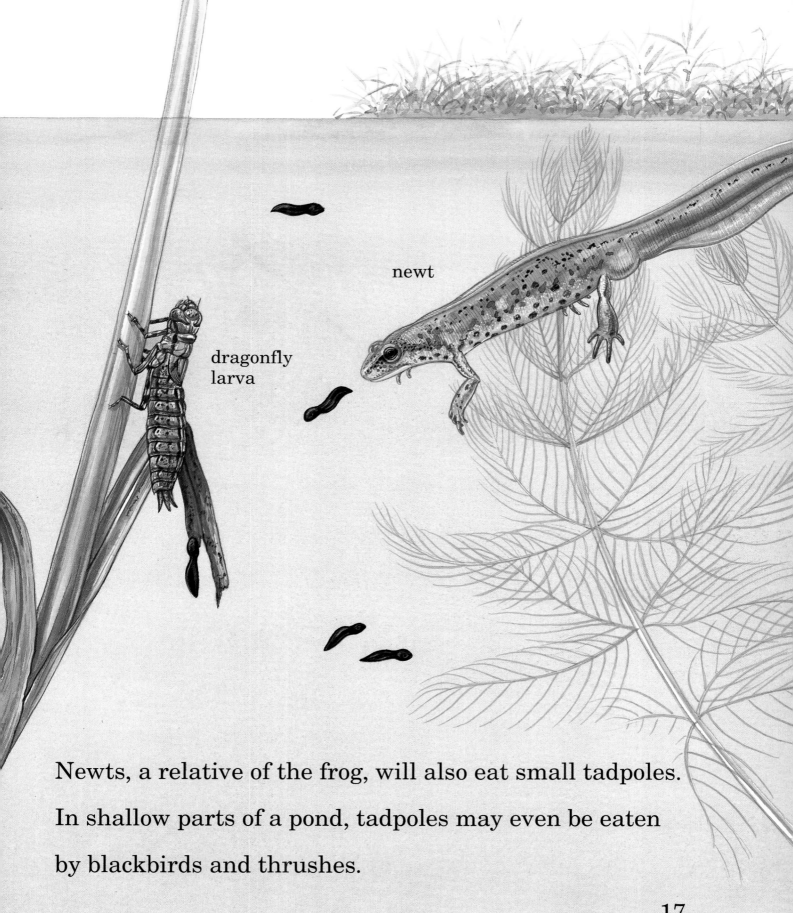

newt

dragonfly
larva

Newts, a relative of the frog, will also eat small tadpoles.

In shallow parts of a pond, tadpoles may even be eaten

by blackbirds and thrushes.

Growing Legs

When the tadpoles are about seven weeks old, they will have grown two back legs. The tadpoles will still eat pond plants, but they will also start to eat other small pond animals.

The tadpoles are now about nine weeks old. Some have grown their front legs and are starting to look like their parents. The tadpoles now have lungs ready for breathing when they leave the water. Their small eyes have also changed so they can now see on land and in the water.

Baby Frogs

When the weather is sunny and warm, the tadpoles grow very quickly. At about twelve weeks old, the tadpoles' tails have disappeared. They look like their parents, but they are still very small.

The baby frogs are now
ready to leave the pond. Like
adult frogs, the young frogs will
stay near water. If they survive, they will
return to the pond in one to three years to breed.

Dangers

Even adult frogs may be eaten by other animals.

The heron stands in the shallow water ready to

grab a frog in its long beak.

Tawny owls sometimes
eat frogs, silently swooping
down from the branch of a
nearby tree.

Frogs may also be eaten by snakes, otters, weasels, and
some ducks.

Disappearing Ponds

Half of the ponds that were around when your parents were children have now disappeared. Some ponds have been drained of water and houses have been built on the land.

People sometimes dump tires, supermarket carts, and other garbage into ponds. Some ponds have also been polluted by dangerous chemicals. When this happens, animals can no longer live in the pond. The water is not safe for the animals to drink.

Backyard Ponds

Backyard ponds are often safe places for frogs to lay eggs and for tadpoles to grow. If you are lucky enough to have one, you can watch some of the stages. If not, ask an adult to take you to a pond in a nearby park or field.

In some parts of the countryside, frogs are becoming rare, but many hundreds of frogs live safely in small park or backyard ponds.

Other Amphibians

There are other types of amphibian that live in the United States. There are several types of toads, including the common toad and the oak toad. The oak toad of the southeastern United States is tiny, no more than one inch long.

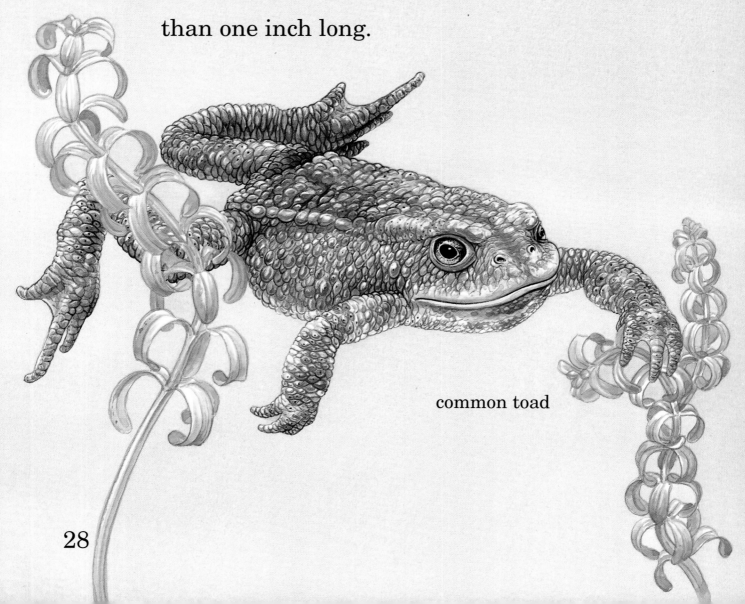

common toad

There are also several types
of salamanders and newts.
Most salamanders and
newts lay their eggs one at
a time or in small clumps.
They hide them under the
leaves of pond plants.

spotted newts

Life of a Frog

1 What is a frog?

2 Hibernation

3 What do frogs eat?

4 Returning to the pond

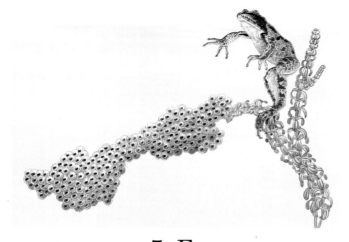

5 Frog spawn

6 The eggs hatch

7 Enemies in the pond

8 Growing legs

9 Baby frogs

10 Dangers

11 Backyard ponds

Glossary

algae Types of plants that grow only in water or on moist ground.

amphibians Animals that are able to breathe in air and water.

gills Organs on the outside of a fish or tadpole's head that enable it to breathe under water.

larvae The very early stage of some animals' lives after they hatch and before they change into adult form.

lungs Organs on the inside of a frog or other animal's body that enable it to breathe air.

Index